LISA'S LINI

Lisa E. Clary

Hats off to you,
Lisa E. Clary
8/2/18

Copyright June 2018
All Rights reserved

Photo Credit
Lisa E. Clary

Copyright June 2018
All Rights reserved
This book, or parts thereof, may not be reproduced in any form without written permission form the Author Lisa E. Clary

Printed in the United States of America

ISBN-10:
1718681534
ISBN-10:
1718681534

Copyright June 2018
All Rights reserved

LISA'S LINES FROM UNDER THE HAT

❋❋❋❋

First & Foremost

I want to thank **GOD** *for giving me the words and for allowing this dream to come to fruition.*

THANKFUL
Lisa E. Clary

In loving Memory

Of

My mother Jane T. Clary
(She was always my biggest fan)

✯✯✯

My dad "Puggie" Clary

✯✯✯

My uncle Archie Tanner

LISA'S LINES FROM UNDER THE HAT

❖❖❖❖

Special Thanks To

My family for their support in my life
Gwen and Gary Painter
Denise and Robbie Williams
Sue and Luby Chandler
Eric Clary
Jordan Sumpter
Randy Cash
Karen Terry

Lisa E. Clary

Welcome to

****

LISA'S LINES FROM UNDER THE HAT

The Bottle
1978

The bottle lay empty, thrown carelessly on the floor.
The room was spinning around me; I groped in this maze for the door.
I had drowned my sorrow in drink; this was my answer to everything.
I never stopped to think.
For a while my problems would be gone: I had found a way out.
The booze would fill my mind; there was nothing to think about.
I stumbled around with my head throbbing in pain,
If only this was a dream, I would never bother with this stuff again.
My problems flooded my mind, they still haunted me.
Oh, no I can't stand it! Is there any way to be free?
I continued to grope around, but I wasn't searching for the door.
Who was I kidding when I said I would do it anymore?
This was my answer and it always would be.
The room spun around and around' it was encircling and trapping me
I reached for another bottle and turned it up to my lips.
I sank to the floor and took a few more sips.
Again I would suffer; my bottle and I alone
What do I care what happens to me
The bottle is my life.
Will it always be?

Children's Games
1979

The song of laughter from the children as they play children's games.
The smile that comes across their face as the ball falls into hands.
The excitement of their voices as they catch you when running.
They are happy.
They play children's games.
The astonishing gasp as the toy becomes alive...in their mind.
The happiness the feel as a story is being read to them.
The delighted face as they win the game.
They are free.
They play children's games
They laugh as the sand flows through their fingers back into the sand box.
Or as the swing climbs higher and higher into the air.
They are children.
They play children's games.
All day they play and at night they sleep.
In their dreams they play children's games.

I Cry Tears for You

I cry tears for what is going on around me.
In a world that is holding us hostage and we struggle to get free.
I see tragedy, disaster and a world falling apart
With floods, earthquakes, fires, and that is just to start
So many things put us to the test every day;
Drugs, crime, and mistakes that get in the way.
I cry tears for you, a lost love, and a sad life of regrets
We experience these misfortunes as a way to never forget.
We hold our own key to how we want to live.
We can choose to seek revenge or we can choose to forgive
I cry tears for you and they stream freely down my face;
But when you see me on the street nothing seems out of place.
I will hold your hand and try to give you a sense of peace
Contentment, happiness, love are things that should never cease
I feel the pain, anger, grief and all your aches.
I will reach out to console and offer what it takes.
I will cry tears for you and try to touch and heal your soul.
I will do whatever it takes to make you feel renewed and whole.
I will listen to your words and guess what they truly mean.
I will always give you a shoulder on which you can lean.
I will be your salvation in your time of need of a friend.
I will lead you ahead and remind where you where you have been
I will be the one you love and always turn too.
I will give you redemption and I will cry tears for you.

Midnight Cowboy
1984

*As he rides through the night
The trail seems long and rough
But he can conquer the wilderness
For his life has always been tough.
The horse sets his pace as he rides through the trees.
The owls sing a night song and the frightened animals flee.
He sits tall up in the saddle with a gun next to his side.
The saddle bags are full for is going to be long ride.
He rides through the night and trees the morning sun.
He is out to get revenge and he won't' stop until the job is done
The days and nights go by and he soon approaches the town.
He is ready for the gunfighter and prepared to shoot him down.
The two men walk towards each other and turn to take ten paces.
The only thing the townspeople can see is the hatred upon the faces.
The two me turn to fire and it's the last and fatal shot.
The sun beats down upon them and it is dusty and very hot.
The bullet hits its mark and there is the echo of a distant train.
The victim falls to the ground: the midnight cowboy never to ride again.*

Fighting the Devil
2015

Satan is chasing me and I am running as fast as I can.
I feel the heat of the flames as he reaches to put out his hand.
But I will not give up; I will not let him take hold.
He is shoving and screaming and trying to get me to fold.
I hear the sounds of evil as he tries to call my name,
But I am not listening or playing his game.
I see the realm of despair that he wants to put me through;
But I won't look hard enough to get caught in something new.
He wants me to take hold of him and follow his road;
But I am on God's path and it is he who is carrying my load.
I am stumbling and falling as the devil gets in my way;
But I get up, and he is going to have to bother me another day.
He is gripping at all that surrounds me;
Pushing me to the edge and he won't let me be.
He is grasping for anything to latch on to my soul,
But God is the one thing that is keeping me whole.
I am crying out to be left alone and moving ahead on my path.
It just angers him more and I feel his wrath.
The flames are growing hotter and bursting around my feet;
He won't give up as he does not want to be beat.
My heart beats faster as I run even harder to get away
I cannot let him catch me or listen to anything that he has to say.
I am running Lord, as fast as I can to get the peace I need,
I will go where you take me and I will follow your lead.
(Continued)

Holding on to your garment hem with fingers locked in a tightened grip.
Reach out for me Lord, and don't let me slip.
I can't hold on much longer and he is closing the gap
If I look back I know I will fall into his trap.
He thinks he will win, but I have a different plan
I call on my Lord and take my own stand.
I will hold steady and stay strong.
With God beside me in this race I can't go wrong.
I call on my Lord and take my own stand.
I will hold steady and stay strong.
With God beside me in this race I can't go wrong.

How Are You?

People ask "how are you today":
You say you are fine because it is what they expect you to say.
But what if you want to say I do not feel my best
Would they care enough to take the load so you can rest?
What if you want to cry and shed lots of tears?
Would they understand and try to alleviate your fears?
What if you felt pains and your body was aching and sore?
Would they know to offer help and do anything more?
What if you told them that your heart was breaking?
Would they see an opportunity that was there for the taking?
If you told them you were lonely and always sad;
Would they make you feel better or just leave you to feel bad?
"How are you today" are words we all toss around.
A conversation starter that holds people hostage to never make a sound.
But they really don't want to know it because it is just word play.
They don't want to know the answer as they go on their way.
But what if you really listened and gave them your ear?
Would it make a difference if they said what they wanted you to hear?
Would it make a difference if they said what they wanted you to hear?
Would it bring a smile and change someone's state of mind?
Is it too hard to show up, pay attention and be a little kind?
"How are you" are three small words we all use each day. (Continued)

If someone gives you true answers let the chips fall where they may.
"How are you" are just little words that we speak and they don't cost a thing:
But being able to really listen; oh the peace to someone that could bring.
Take the time to hear exactly what they mean, even if cuts like a knife
That moment of caring and compassion just may change a life.
It could be yours or it could be theirs;
But being there in the moment shows that someone really cares.

Just Random Thoughts

The facade is cracking.
The fractures are splintering.
The structure is crumbling.
The dust is swirling.
The space is empty and barren.

About Poetry

Poetry is something that comes from the heart;
It does not always have to rhyme right from the start.
Words should flow as they come to mind;
There are different ways to write and different kinds.
Sonnets, haikus, couplets and limericks;
So many forms, themes and writing gimmicks
They should give you a reason to think and find a voice
The versions you read should be your choice
They tell a story and leave you wanting more
Or say so much in a few words in tales of lore
From the pens of great poets of years long ago
From Browning to Frost to Whitman and Poe
Lines of words that you long to understand
Turn into pages from Shakespeare with the flick of a hand.
Poetry is what the writer sees as verse that tells how they feel.
It is spiritual, emotional and expresses what is real.
No one else has to get it or have it make any sense
The language they use can be very intense
Read it as you want to as it what it is to one's own eyes
See what you see, hear what you hear and find where the meaning lies
It can be long or short and whatever words that say what they mean
They can paint a picture of a visual scene
It depends on the pace and rhythm in which you read
It is done in its own time and at a paced speed
Poetry is something that you get used to understanding in time
And the words do not always have to rhyme
This one is written this way because it is what readers are used to
But for defining, explaining, or comprehending, I leave all that up to you.

Glory

I am not perfect, never claimed to be;
Just want to be the person God meant me to be.
We strive to meet his expectations knowing we will fail.
Christ is the chosen perfect one and we follow his trail.
He gave all for us to be able to have a good life to live.
What he asks of us is not too much too give.
Believe in his words and follow them the best we can,
Remember he has it all laid for us in his own special plan.
It may not be what we want, but it will be what we need;
Just believe and follow and let him take the lead.
All good things will come in his time and be right for you;
We just have to be faithful and trust him in all we do.
He is the answer to our struggles, grief and pain.
He will come to our rescue again and again.
He holds the key to a fuller life of joy and peaceable love;
In our time of need we need to trust the lord above?
Read and follow his word: the bible is the true story.
   Say a prayer and be sure to give God all the glory.

Last Ride

Dedicated to my Uncle Archie D. Tanner who rode the rails for 30 years

All aboard for a wild ride as that runaway train speeds down the track.
No way to break and stop or even turn back:
Set to crash and derail from the long iron beams
Toppling everything around as nothing is as it strong as it seems.
It seems as if the wheels are metaphors for life all around.
As nothing is the same and we search for something not to be found.
We can't change history so we make it easy to disappear and erase.
That train is squealing on those tracks at a very fast pace.
Leaning into curves riding close to the ledge:
Always a force that seems about to go over the edge.
That engine is pulling a mighty heavy load that is the key to the past.
The whistle sounds an echoing tune in the wind as it struggles to last.
The momentum of the times pushes it through a tunnel that is dark;
Leaving behind a smoke trail that fades away not leaving a mark.
History has become baggage that the world struggles to unload;
Making it seem as if there are no debts to be paid and nothing is left that is owed.
The trainmen walking the tracks, coupling, switching, riding the caboose at the end,
Watching what is coming up ahead as it passes around the bend. (Continued)

Passengers, freight, animals all ride in different cars to the local depot
The engineers letting all know that they are here as they listen to the whistle blow.
Times of the past as these reminders fade away to make room for other things.
But who knows what the future holds and what changes it may bring?
It will hide the signs that link the world to the past and how others had to live.
Making their own mark to pass along as they had nothing else to give.
All aboard to a new junction, new station, and a railroad crossing sign left on the side.
Step up to the platform, board the train, listen for the all clear and enjoy one last wild ride.

True Colors
© October 2017

When you see the true colors of what is around you,
You realize that all is not as it seems and so much is not true.
The pure hearts you envision are suddenly shades of grey.
The burnt reds and oranges of the setting sun darken the day.
The black darkness of night encompasses the light that shines
You see things differently and now it becomes blurred lines.
The true colors of those around will soon come out;
They harbor an evil will that lurks deep as you want to understand what it is about.
The hearts of those around you are not what they should be.
They hold thoughts of hate, hurt, anger and more you can't see
People push you to say and do what is not your true being.
The true color of who they are is now what you are seeing:
Deceit, lies, and telling so many tall tales;
Waiting and hoping that it sets you up so it all fails.
They sneak and creep around you before they make their move
Waiting for the right moment to show they have something to prove.
Jealousy rears its ugly head when others see you reaping rewards and praise,
They will set out to sabotage you in any and all ways.
True colors come out when they can't be the center of all things.
(Continued)

They become the one who whines and don't care what feelings they bring.
Green with envy they set out to bring you down.
They don't care who they hurt or who is around.
True colors always come out and they will see the real you.
You can't hide two faces for so long and they will reveal all that is true.
True colors that are a mirage of what they really should be.
When they set out to fool you into seeing what they want you to see.
Don't be fooled by the fake and phony actions and words they speak.
They want you to feel let down so they catch you when you are weak.
True colors will come out when someone doesn't get their way.
Don't get caught in their trap; just don't take the time to play.
The game will not end well if you let them get ahead.
Step back and let them show their colors instead.
All will be revealed as the show they put on comes to an end.
Then they will only have their own true colors to defend.

Random

The moon hangs low in the sky, lighting a pathway that will take you to day break.
Shining down on all those who sleep peacefully in their beds as well as those who are awake.
The mysteries of what lies beyond the bright round ball are not what they seem.
Whatever really lies beyond will be what you see tonight only as you dream.
The tales I tell are life lessons learned.
The words I speak or write bring them to life.
The beliefs I hold keep me true to myself.
The thoughts I have are mine alone.
No one can think for me, speak for me or tell me what to believe.
Those are things that are only achieved through learning who you are as a person;
Not who someone else wants you to be.
The feelings
I have can run deep for hurt, pain, anger, hate, but most of all for love.
Love should be the one feeling that is constant during all the rest.
Love for yourself, love for the others who may cause the other feelings
The prayers I say are for things that make life better for all.
The life I live is one to honor those who have gone ahead and those who are here with me.
But most of all I am a child of God and I live for his love and grace.

*****

This page is when I have no words to speak or write. It happens from time to time and I must learn to listen to the mind, body, heart and soul and the voice of God!

*****

Are You Listening GOD?

*Are you listening god
Can you really hear when I pray?
Am I saying the right words that you want to hear? Or
are mental thoughts getting in the way
Can you hear me God when I am in tears?
Trying to talk to you with signs of heartbreak on my face
I am not always on my knees when I ask for help
Do hear my words from any and every place
Do I ask for the right things to better my life and heart
Does it matter if I folded my hands or bow my head when
the words come?
Does it matter how I talk to you and even where I start.
Can you feel the pain as my soul cries out for peace?
I need a calming of my body of and mind
Will the screaming in my head ever begin to cease
Are you listening God it seems I want to yell it out.
I can't see you, your expressions or hear any sounds.
I want to know it is working and never have any doubt.
But is all in your time and I know I may have to wait
To hear you tell me that my answer is upon me
And any plan you have will always be great.
I am here lord, giving it all to you the best I know how
Are you listening God;
I am yours in spirit, and mind, heart and I give you all
the power.*

Words on Paper

When my mind is filled with random words and thoughts I tend to write;
It does really mean anything if I am up writing in the middle of the night.
Just have to put it out of my mind and clear up my head.
When I can't sleep, the words all tend to come while I am in bed.
I spend all day with words as part of my job and my life
It is not unusual that darkness is when they cause me the most strife.
Too much quiet time or even too much noise and sound
Can wreak havoc with the restlessness that encompasses all around.
It could be a word, a sentence or a line someone says that may take hold
And it sends my mind into a rush of thoughts that must now be told.
They may not all make sense and they don't have to rhyme.
They just have to mean something when I write them at the time
No one else has to understand what they are trying to say.
It is just how I handle my stress; it is just my way.
They have to be released from my overflowing mind.
It is my calm, my peace and my inner soul that I find.
They are just words that often take over when my mind is racing around.
They spin out of control until I release them before I become unwound.
They don't always have any hidden meanings for others to look for.
They are just words that need to be written before there are many more. (Continued)

Because I know there will be at some point at night, or when I am stressed.
But I will put them down on paper and for this talent I will consider myself blessed.

Random

If love is euphoria and hatred takes you to the depths of hell, how do get euphoria back from the depths of hell once you have reached that level?

Come As You Are

My door is always open so come as you are;
To find peace, ease and comfort, you don't have to go far.
There will be challenges and trials you will struggle to meet;
But you won't give up or admit to defeat.
I am watching over you and guiding your path on the way:
The bumps you come upon will be lessons in your life each day.
Come as you are as there are no limitations here.
I will be sure you will know there is no reason to fear.
The doors to my home are open to you when you have something to say.
Come as you are to the altar and bow your head to pray.
I will be listening to your words as well as your heart;
Take your time as I am always here whenever you are ready to start.
I will not judge or place too many expectations on you.
I will guide the way to help you decide what you need to do.
Come as you are whether happy, sad, lonely, tired, rich or poor.
My home is always welcoming so walk through the door.
My arms are outstretched to embrace the person that I see before me.
I am your Lord and savior and I know your true soul.
Some come as you are and let me lead and your hand I will hold.
Follow me to my treasures in heaven and you will find peace.
The joy that is there forever will go on and never cease
Come as you are as I am the heavenly father and I welcome you to sit near my throne
My door stands open so come on in and you will no longer be alone. (Continued)

*Come as you are as you no longer have to roam.
You may enter here and rest now as you have found your eternal home.*

Random

Love and hate.
If you hit the hatred emotion can you ever get back to love?
Probably not as easily as going from love to hate.
Love is good and hate is evil.
Evil is a lot harder to get over.

The End Game

What happens in the end game when you are all alone?
Will there be anyone to stop by or call you on the phone?
Will anyone check on you to see if you are ok or not?
Will they know that you are holding on with everything you have got?
Will they care if you have troubles that maybe you can't fix:
Or will they think only of themselves not wanting to bother and get in the mix.
What happens in the end game as things become harder to do?
You don't mention it as means they will have sorrow or pity for you.
Will anyone watch your door, the movement and the lights?
Or will they just pass on by and think all is fine and all is right.
Will they know the quiet and sadness that may rest within the walls?
When no one checks in, stops by or even calls.
What happens in the end game when tears are cried more often than not?
When cries for help are ignored and silence is all you have got.
When the doors are closed and lights are out and quiet is all around;
When it seems as if the busyness of life has left you and has let you down.
When the world closes you out and no one checks in to ask are you;
It is all about the outside and you are trapped in body mind and spirit too.
What happens in the end game when the world realizes you are left out? (Continued)

Will you be missed for longer than a .minute or is there any doubt?
When the darkness shuts down the light;
Do you have anyone left to fight?
What happens in the end game when you are really gone for good?
Would anyone notice it before too much time passes if they could.
The end game can come slowly or it can come fast.
Just pray the game is good to you and does not drag on and last;
Hope there is someone there for you in the light and it is again your time to shine.
Someone to offer caring thoughts and someone to tell that all will be fine.
The heavenly father is the one to reach out to so just call out his name:
His hand is outstretched for you as he opens his door to help you finish playing the end game.

The Pew
2014

Sunday morning church is just an hour of your time each week:
But it is an everyday peace and comfort that we should set out to seek.
If we don't find time for God, will he find time for us when we call his name?
Somehow an hour in return for what he offers us does not match up the same.
A Sunday morning pew sitter, always there for others to see:
But what happens when they leave; who do they turn out to be?
We sing the hymns of praise and bow our heads to pray.
But do we really hear the words of what the minister has to say?
Do we make a difference each day and practice what we preach?
Or is being a total Christian, dedicated to the Lord, far out of our reach?
Who on this earth do we need to impress, for they can't save our soul:
Only God can give us peace and make our lives seem whole.
He knows what is in our hearts and how each day will play out.
He will give us all the answers when we have questions or doubt.
It does not matter what day of the week or the time of the day.
He will listen to our fears, troubles, and worries and hear what we say.

It does not make a difference if you are sitting on the church pew or on your knees anywhere, he will stop to listen to you. (Continued)
If we don't find time for God, will he find time for us?
Will we keep believing and knowing he is the one to trust?
Will we take him with us and keep him in our heart;
When those who don't believe try to tear our faith apart?
Will we stand up for the love of our lord and what we know is true? Or will we be that Sunday morning Christian that only fills the pew?

Oh, How We Grieve

Oh, how we grieve for those not here:
Even though they are in place where there is no fear.
We revisit the past and wonder where did time go?
We wonder if you knew that we loved you so.
Oh, how we grieve for those we have lost:
Wondering if we did all we could for you at any cost.
We remember the good times and the joy that you brought
All the things you did and the lessons you taught.
Oh, how we grieve for those we love:
Even though we know they are safe in heaven above.
We think about all the things you have done for us as we grew.
Not because we asked, but because you wanted to.
Oh, how we grieve for those that mean so much to us all
You were always around to catch us when we would fall.
We think of you often and remember your smile.
If you could only be here again for just a little while.
Oh, how we grieve for those who touch our lives in some way.
How much you will be missed, words can never say.
You were always there when needed through the years:
Waiting quietly to laugh with us or to wipe our tears.
Oh, how we grieve for those who made such an impact in our life.
The grief is agony and cuts life a knife.
We will remember you with respect, kindness, love and devotion.
But right now we are all so filled with unbelievable shock and emotion.
Oh, how we grieve for those taken from us and a life made so brief
We don't understand it; there is hurt, pain and so much grief. (Continued)

But, oh the love you had in your life from the beginning to the end.
You were the best person, brother, father, uncle and friend.
Oh how we grieve and though we may now be apart.
All the love you gave and received came straight from the heart.
Our memories will live on and become our treasures to hold and share
Until we see you on the other side waiting patiently for us there.
Oh how we grieve for one who has gone to a better home to rest.
We take solace in the knowing that you are at peace and blessed.

Cry

Sometimes the tears just want to fall and flow;
Rolling down my cheeks moist and slow.
Thoughts that trigger the glistening drops;
Fill my mind and just won't stop.
Feeling alone and so unhappy and sad;
Just moments of misery and feeling bad.
Moments remembered that bring those tears;
No soothing words can calm the fears.
They hold my mind hostage and I want to hide;
But I just try to hold good thoughts bottled up inside.
Even though I feel empty and broken like glass;
I weep until the despair I hold will pass.
The sobs keep coming and my body breaks;
I give in to the crying for as long as it takes.
Refreshing the soul, looking for some peace;
I know sooner or later the anguish will cease.
I will stop the tears and regain my strength.
It lasts as long as it needs to as there is no certain time length.
The heart will know when I need to let go and cry.
I will take the time to do so as hurt doesn't lie.
The emotions I feel are mine and I will feel as I need;
Until I am spent and empty and all feelings cede.
The tears I cry leave steaks and a wet trace;
The only signs that I have cried are left on my face.

Random

There is a beast that rages within all of us. Be very careful about how and where you unleash it.

On My Knees

I am on my knees Lord; my head bowed to pray.
I need to talk to you about the devil in my day.
He is working hard to get me to do things that go against you;
But I'm fighting back and using your strength to get me through.
So many things I question about those who don't put you first
I try to live right yet the devil is doing his worst,
Tempting, testing, and pulling me all around;
But I am trying to stand tall and hold my ground.
I know you won't let me fall as I get close to the edge;
I may stumble and lose my balance, but I won't let go of the ledge.
I will hold on to the threads of your garment even the tattered hem.
The evil spirits may be doing their best to dance around to get me to join them;
But I dance to the beat of the heavenly drums and angels that sing.
I have my own spiritual guide that holds me and takes me under his wing;
As I follow the path that takes me to so many greater things.
I will welcome the outcome no matter what it brings.
I am on my knees Lord, as I pray for me to be the best person I can be.
I need to let you be my warrior to fight and make the devil flee.
My soul cries out for peace of mind and keeping love in my heart;
Forgiving and moving on is sometimes the hardest part.
Thank you Lord for listening and hearing my thoughts and pleas. (Continued)

I give it all to you now to handle and will hold onto my faith as I rise from my knees.
I am still hanging on as I go about my life and continue through the day.
I believe in Jesus Christ, my Savior, and when I need him again I will be on my knees to pray.

Around The Throne

My holidays will be different this year as I will celebrate from heaven above;
With those gone before me that I miss and love.
The songs will be sung in tune and lights brighter all around.
I will watch over you and many blessings for you will abound.
I will feel your hearts beat and know they are sad;
But I am in a better place, so please don't feel bad
I have no pain and angel wings made of gold.
I am now in a place where I will never grow old.
.I miss you all but God is now holding my hand.
He had his reasons and he had his plan.
It is not for you to understand or try to figure out;
You just have to trust him and in him have no doubt.
I can see all those that were a part of my life over the years;
Sharing our memories, love and walking away from fears.
I will be celebrating a different kind of Christmas so don't cry for me
I'll be touching your lives from the place I was not afraid to go and wanted to be
I will be rejoicing from my heavenly home and   not ever alone
I am with the angels and am now celebrating and dancing around the throne.

Sunday Morning
Lisa E. Clary ©

The Lord said, "Welcome to my home;
A place where you are never alone.
The door is always open to who all who need me.
I am here for you with prayers and blessings for thee.
Come Sunday morning, a man stands at the back, not coming in the door.
The Lord said, my child, what is it that keeps you away, what are you looking for?
I cannot enter, he answered for I do not have the proper shoes or clothes.
That is alright my child, as long you are covered, God does not care much about all those.
As long as you are dressed in faith and love, you are welcome here.
The man answered, I will take the back pew then so others will feel no fear.
That is fine my child. God does not care where you sit;
As long as you listen to his word, hear what is said and truly believe in it.
Again he said, Thank you Lord, I will heed the word and praise him in my thoughts.
And the Lord said: Oh my child, you may sing and rejoice in hymns that we have all been taught.
Make a joyful noise and give God all the Glory in song.
For when you sing about his love, no note is ever wrong.
When you bow your head to pray and ask for forgiveness of sin.
Just remember, he already knows what you have done and where you have been.
He passes no judgment when you come into his house, no matter how you are dressed.
He is waiting with open arms and wants you to feel loved and blessed. (Continued)

He does not worry about where you sit or how you lift your voice.
He only cares, my child, that you made a spiritual choice;
To have faith, trust and hope and believe in God's true love.
And heart is always full of God's holy word and blessings from our savior above.
It is not just for Sunday, but every day of the week and every hour of the day.
You should know he is walking beside you every step of the way.
The door is always open; my house is your home to pray, to fill your heart and soul.
Come in my child; take a seat and listen, because the word of God never gets old.

Puppets

We are all puppets in a world gone mad:
Being manipulated by others and forgetting what we had.
Dancing strings attached to movement at another's will;
Pretending to be free but the connection is there still.
Can't let go, can't be released and can't be free;
Moving through the motion as a pawn in a game.
Nothing seems to change, yet nothing stays the same.
How do we cut the ties of a world gone insane?
As it plays with our mind to find out what it is that we gain.
Hands that move and create the motion of what we do;
The sound of voices in our heads that makes us wonder who is who.
Time moves on and the world keeps on turning.
We keep asking questions and just keep on learning.
But we are still puppets in a world that is gone mad.
We can't really make a difference if we can't go back to what we had.
We just keep dancing in place going nowhere fast.
If we don't cut the strings how long will the hold last.
Time to break free and do our own thing
No longer someone else's toy or their puppet on a string.

No Peace

There is no peace, no calm; only turmoil
There is chaos, havoc and a soul dark with despair.
There is no light, no joy, and no color;
Only gray that is shaded between black and white.
There is no hope, no trust or reaching for the light.
Only a hole filled with despair and desolate, empty space.
There is no solace in knowing there are things out of your reach.
No matter how long or far you search out it will just be out of your grasp.
There is no peace of mind, soul, heart or body.
Just a deep sense of loss of something you will never find.
Something you will never know, feel or understand.
It is just a blank spot of nothingness that leaves you wanting more of something.
It will only get bigger and deeper and never get filled.
And it will only be loneliness, distress and a heaviness of your being.
What will be on the other side of misery, hopelessness and a tortured mind?
Quiet rest, solace, graces a place to lay it all out.
Or will it just all stay the same as the world plays with your mind.
And you seek words, wisdom and comfort for what is playing out in life.
But there really is no peace or calm or a method to sedate your soul.
Only your connection to God, prayer and faith can bring down the demons and defeat the devil in this battle.

In The Dark

Close your eyes and see the darkness of the night;
There is no color, no forms, shape or light.
In the dark there is nothing but black:
Filling a space and you can't keep track.
What moves around you can only be heard.
You can move forward on a spoken word.
You feel your way and react to touch;
In the dark you don't see much.
Close your eyes and listen to your mind;
What can you hear: what do you hope to find?
You reach out to find nothing there;
Empty space filled with holes that are bare.
You see nothing and you can only guess;
What hides in the blackness and causes unrest.
Close your eyes and you are all alone
The room around you develops a different tone.
Nothing to see but a huge, blank space:
You want to open your eyes just in case.
Deep, cold nothingness all around you;
Close your eyes and there is nothing to see or do.
You are in your own world and lost to the night:
Remember the visions you have when there is sight.
But you can have a dark heart and spirit as well.
Don't be entrapped and fall under that spell.
See the light and open your eyes to a brighter day;
Let the sun and brightness in so it can lead the way.
Follow the light as your eyes take in all the sights:
Soon you will close your eyes again to the darkness of night.

In My Head

My mind is filled with words 24 hours a day.
Thought or ideas I have to get out of the way.
Have to write them all down to clear my head;
Hoping somewhere and someway will get read.
Too many words about so many things:
Let's see what comes out, let's see what it brings.
Always thinking about what to say;
Putting it on paper hopefully makes it go away.
The flurry of words just keeps floating around;
Until I make them make sense in how they sound.
Got to clear them from my mind and head
Just so many words, so much to be said.
They are my thoughts until I write them down for others to see
Just have to get them out there and set them free.
My head is filled with so much stuff that I have to say
I just write all down to get it out of the way.

A Prayer for Peace
November 2015 ©

*Dear Lord I hope I come out of this stronger than before:
My mother was our strength whenever we entered her door
But now that she is gone, how can I be the strong when one it hurts so bad.
I know she is in heaven with grandma, her brother and my dad.
But it is hard to understand why she left this earth so soon and fast
With little to time to fight and know that those few short days would be her last.
I don't want to be bitter and angry as she would not want that for any of us
But it is hard to understand and sometimes we have to question the God we are supposed to trust.
My tears flow freely as I write these words to get them off my mind.
I am searching for a peace Lord, which I hope you will help me find.
I know I am not the only one that prays for answers in a time of need and loss.
But prayer and faith is the only thing that is free and comes at no cost.
She was such a strong Christian and held onto her beliefs every day.
Maybe you needed her more Lord to show someone else the way.
She was not afraid and was ready to greet you Lord, but she had to leave us behind.
She did not want to and we promised her would be strong so as to ease her mind.
But this is really hard, (Lord, and we are doing the best we can to get through. (Continued)*

And trying to not be angry and resentful is touching everything we say and do.
I pray for your guidance and healing hands to make this easier as I write these words down.
It is the only way I know to set these feelings free and is a release for me I have found.
My mother would read them all and be my biggest fan no matter what she would read.
But she would never want me to question God because he would always meet my need.
My heart is open Lord and I don't want to become someone I am not.
Even for a short time as I struggle to get through, my sense of who I am is really I have got.
The person she raised to love, to give to others and to always work for a living.
She would want us all to keep that because she was an example of loving and giving.
Well, I need you now, Lord, to get through this trying time, today and every day.
Lord, I hope you are listening as this prayer is what I pray.

Anger and Hate

*Anger can make you say or do ugly things.
Hate devours love and all that it brings.
The feelings of anguish as you wrestle them,
From the depths of your soul they fester on the brim.
Waiting to bring the heat and fire as the two unite.
Bring the boiling emotions out to fight.
Flowing over into words, emotions and actions;
That feed off the so many other feelings that you can't gain traction.
The anger and hate so volatile that it builds to high steam:
Simmering close enough to the top that you can't hold it in or make it stop.
Ready to combust and explode like a fireworks show;
That lights up the night with streaming colors and a hot glow.
Hate and anger can turn a pure heart of gold to black.
Leaving it sore and hurting and wondering how to get back;
To the love and goodness that use to be there.
Until you are forced to feed off others meanness and ugly ways.
Your own response festering and smoldering for days and days.
And it seeped into your own soul and it now runs deep
It can hurt you physically and make you weep.
How do you get back the love and the light?
The glow of goodness and the will to always do right
Walk away from the evil around you that leads you astray.
Ask for forgiveness for yourself and the one who holds you at bay
Pacing around you, grabbing, reaching and pulling you in
(Continued)*

Taking you to a place you don't understand and have never been.
Anger and hate are powerful emotions that rage down deep inside.
From low depths that are kept in a cage
Once that door is open and they bubble to the top
How do you get back to peace and make it all stop?
Turn to God and remember his mercy and grace:
Anger and hate will fade away and it you will be left with only a trace.
Face down the devil that taunts you and brings you to the brink.
Don t let him win as you are much stronger than you think.
The power of prayer and a deep faith will bring you back
From the depths of anger and hate to being back on track
Fill your mind with good thoughts and just wait
You will soon be able to defeat all the anger and hate.

Prayer of Need
2015

Dear Lord I hope you can hear me as I bow my head to pray.
Sometime I just don't have the words or know what to say.
I am seeking answers and I am turning to you;
To lead and guide my path in all I say and do.
I need to feel your presence as I travel down life's road,
I need you with me to carry the burden and heavy load.
I can't do this all on my own and need the helping hand;
I will hold tightly to it and beside you I will stand.
My faith has been tested but you did not dessert me in my time of need.
No matter where I turned to go, you took over the lead.
I felt your grace surrounding me when I was I was searching for peace for my soul.
Only you can pick up the shattered pieces and restore them to being whole.
I am trying to listen and move forward with a renewed sense of well-being;
Learning to feel, hear, listen and opening my eyes to be all seeing.
To know that you are always near even when I am unsure you are there;
Never judging, but letting me know the load is yours to bear.
As the cross you carried was to clear us all of our sin and shame.
We are children of God and we should all remember that we all should praise your name.
As I come to the end of my prayer I feel a sense of relief,
As all it takes is a little faith, love of the Lord and holding true to a belief.

The Gifts
December 10, 2011

The gift of love on earth is a treasure to behold.
It can't be bought by diamonds or gold.
The gift of compassion is from the heart
Felt so deeply from the very start
The gift of faith is true to the soul
Nothing to touch, nothing to hold
The gift of laughter comes from joy down deep.
Laugh hard, but don't be afraid to weep.
The gift of peace comes from a spiritual life
No worries, no troubles, realities or strife.
The gift of strength, comes from having all these things
To lift you up to let you spread your wings.
All these gifts are free to give during any season.
Do so willingly and for no reason.
The gift of Christmas comes from heaven above.
It comes from God's heart as he shares his love.
Be a gift giver and share all that is good about you.
But most of all is true to yourself and others in all that you do.

Be the One

Be the person others look up to.
Be kind, gracious and humble in all you do.
Have a good heart and soul and hands that do good deeds.
Be the one that takes the lead.
Take the time to make good things happen when you can
Do it with a smile and a helping hand.
Be the one to teach others patience, strength and gratitude
Take the extra moment to make the difference with a better attitude.
Smile and laugh and be the one that others rely on and trust.
Honesty, truth and confidence are a must.
Be the person who can get any job done.
The person others want to be like: Be the one.

Say What You Mean

Say what you mean and mean what you say;
Don't keep us guessing your thoughts all day.
Make things happen but include others, too;
Don't take all the credit for something you didn't do.
Don't always think your way is the only one:
More ideas together can get the job done.
Take a step to the side and give others a little space;
We all need to breathe without someone always in our face.
We need to listen and to be able to hear;
But bullying for your way will help turn a deaf ear.
No one wants to be pushed to think like one and all.
Too much having it your way will back others up against a wall.
They will eventually fight back and you won't know what to do.
You have to learn to give and take a little too.
So get over the ego trips and the know it all talk.
It will make others just take their own stand and away they will walk.
Say what you mean and mean what you say.
Talking out both sides of your mouth is just not nice on any day.
Speak your mind and make the words count.
Truth is always the best way and can come in any amount.
Say the words that that are in your head and heart.
Tell me something good; you just have to get a start.
Say what you think and say what you feel:
In today's world it is all about keeping it real.
You think who cares if words hurt those all-around;
As long as you look good and hold your ground.
Right or wrong, it means nothing anymore
(Continued)

*As long as you dish it out they will come back for more.
Scared to mean what you say and say what you mean;
Just get it all out, say the words and just come clean.
Speak it loud and make it all clear;
Say what it is and say the words without fear.
We have the freedom to speak without others getting all out of joint.
So stop talking and give others a chance to make a point.
Say what you mean and mean what you say;
And just make it easier to get through the day.
But if you can't play fair then expect what you get in return.
A little bit of payback will be a good lesson for you to learn.
Act like you know something but never tell all you know
A little mystery will make them wonder and you will see how crazy they will go.*

Secrets and Lies

Secrets can come out and change so many things.
Lies can do damage that opens up issues and what they bring.
Secrets can hold you hostage for so very long.
Lies can destroy those who may have done no wrong.
Secrets hurt those who hold on to them for reasons unknown.
Lies can bring down powerful people when you throw the first stone.
Secrets make you afraid to speak your mind or heart.
Lies can wreak havoc and tear lives apart.
Secrets show you have something to hold over someone.
Lies will give you the upper hand until they unravel and come undone.
Secrets are the thoughts that you hold close to the vest.
Lies are told for the undoing of others to put them to the test.
Secrets that are kept hidden are the ones who serve others well.
Lies spoken out of turn can bring others into pure hell.
Secrets should be kept and not used as a bargaining chip.
Lies are a twisted truth that comes from the tongue just waiting to slip.
Secrets should stay hidden as they are told in trust.
Lies are words that haunt those that are honorable and just.
Secrets are the same as lies if you mix them all up to save your own skin.
Lies halt the game and make it where you can't win.
Hold the secrets and never talk lies that hurt just because you can.
Secrets and lies do not necessarily make you a woman or man. (Continued)

So many with secrets and so many tell lies;
If you tell the secrets that you know would that be wise?
If you stop the lies and make it all about truth in words;
Would that make up for all the trouble that was stirred?
Secrets and lies can only hurt all in the end
Be sure you know what you are doing before you even begin.

Time

*Time is the one thing that we never have enough of;
and affects everything we do in daily life including how
we love.
We can't see it, touch it or feel it, but is the one thing we
need each day
Time to get things done, time to live, laugh, love and play.
Material things can't soothe your soul, hold a hand or
wrap arms around you.
Time is the only thing that is fleeting in all that we do.
Don't waste too much of it on things that don't mean a lot:
Take advantage of what is around us and appreciate
what you have got.
You could be holding someone close, kissing someone's
lips and loving that special someone.
It is with them you need the time and we all want more
when it is all said and done.
No one wants to be alone when the end is near.
You want someone close and one you hold dear.
Sometimes we realize what we missed and it is way too
late.
To get back those precious moments that we made
someone wait.
Too many moments are lost on such trivial things as time
passes by;
Moments we can't get back no matter how hard we try.
Don't let little things distract from sharing, loving and
giving.
In the end it is all that makes life really worth living.
A hand to hold, a smile, and a heart that offers it all at
free will.
To the one closet to them; the one that makes their world
stand still.
Time is too fleeting as the hours tick by too fast:
Time to move forward and stop living in the past.
(Continued)*

Time is not on our side and it is not a close friend.
The lack of it and it sneaking up on us will get us in the end.
Don't miss out on something because time is slipping away.
By the second, the hour and so quickly by the day.
Reach out and grab what is left of it and make each day count for something
Look for love and laughter and see what it all will bring.
No one wants to be alone today, tomorrow or in the end.
So make the most of each moment and the time that you spend.
Hold on to those who make your life better and give you comfort and more
Peace, joy, happiness, contentment and love are all we are really living for.

Power Play

*Everyone wants to be a power player and run the show
Even if there are so many things they don't really know.
On the fast track to go full speed ahead
Not caring who gets hurt or where their feet will tread.
It is all about looking good and making a name
To them it is all about just being the winner of the game.
It is the "me" generation who wants it to happen right now.
They don't think about what it really takes or even know how.
Show me the money and send me on my way
Make it happen the way they want it to and make it happen today.
Don't think about the consequences and what it will change
Doesn't matter how it turns out or what it means long range.
Follow the leader to the end of the road, waiting on someone else to help carry the load.
Standing on the sidelines is just not in the cards
Jumping off the edge and the landing will be hard.
Egos and self-importance enhance the adrenalin rush
As all fight for the top and don't care who they crush.
The world is theirs for the taking or so they seem to think
But so many things change before they even blink.
Survival of the fittest as they steal another's dream
It is too late to off a challenge and too late to redeem.
Push and shove and move on as you are blocking my path.
If you are not fast enough you will feel the wrath.
They don't really see what the future holds for all
They just want to be in charge and make the last call.
Just keep in mind as you make those steps to the top.
There is always someone out there behind to see that you also stop. (Continued)*

*It is just a fleeting moment of I have had my own way,
Because times continue to change and tomorrow is a new day.
Those who follow will do the very same to you as you watch your back.
They will be the ones that will set things on a different track.
Oh wait, that is what you set out to do and now you are under attack.
Suddenly it all seems pointless and the changes you made now fades to black.*

Mother

You should pay homage to your mother every day;
Show respect, take care of, love and obey.
They hold you closest to the heart.
From the day you are born, they set you on your life path right from the start.
They take care of your needs whether sick or well, morning or night;
They give you courage, confidence and teach you wrong from right.
They will go to the ends of the earth for you;
Sacrifice their own needs to see that you have all that you do.
You can never do any wrong in their eyes as their love runs deep.
They will laugh with you, protect you and hold you when you weep.
A mother's arms will reach out to you near and far.
They feel your struggles no matter where you are.
A mother's love can never be matched and is like no other around
It is where safety, security and compassion can always be found.
Take the time to give her respect and hold her most dear.
Do it every day and not just one day a year.
To those who hold a special place in your life, be sure to honor them always
Give them the love they deserve today and all days.
You only get one mother, where under her heart you had to rest.
Everything she has done for you has always been for the best.
To my mom, who is special to me in every way?
I send her my love and wish her a Happy Mother's Day!

No Boundaries

It seems that there are not any boundaries anymore.
Nothing to hold any one in and they go straight for the core.
No edges, no limits, no barricades; just a drop off free for all;
Every man for himself as they slither around the invisible wall
Grabbing at whatever they want and what they think is theirs;
Turn a blind eye and a deaf ear as if nobody cares.
No boundaries for doing what is fair and right.
Just pushing forward with their hard headed might.
They run over those that get in the way.
They don't care who is hurt or who has to pay.
No boundaries for caring what is really going on around them;
Just forging ahead acting on any old whim.
As long as they have what they want they see nothing wrong.
Taking, laughing, and ignoring the truth as they go along.
No boundaries for how their actions make others feel;
Not caring that what happens to others is very real.
The world is open for those who pilfer and take what others worked for.
They think they have the right and all they want is more.
No boundaries, no walls, no heart, no soul, just a nothing feeling.
Their actions and reactions can leave others reeling.
An empty facade with nothing to give and nothing inside.
Just push forward with no conscious and no pride.
They have no concept of what life is really all about.
No boundaries to hold them in so they're always searching for a way out. (Continued)

But they are really trapped in their own little world and empty mind?
Waiting for others to do the job to see what they can find.
They step up and take what is not theirs to have and they did not earn.
Overstepping boundaries that should never be crossed at every turn.
It means nothing to them to try to hurt others to get ahead;
But they need to know where they are being led.
Not seeing they are losing on their own ground
Are you going to let it happen by just standing around?
No boundaries means the game is open to all who want to play.
What happens when the boundaries finally hold you in to stay?
Caught in your own trap with no way to set yourself free.
Locked in, no way out, and time to think about being alone with no boundary.

Hats

I wear hats of many colors, shapes and styles.
I have them everywhere stored in piles.
They are my trademark and make me stand out in a crowd.
They are a part of who I am and I stand proud.
I started wearing them to help with migraines.
They were supposed to help protect me from the pain;
That could be caused by wind, bright sun and cold.
Doctor said to do it, so and I did as I was told.
They became an everyday thing and the collection began.
Buying them everywhere was part of my plan.
They match my outfits and I can change the bands on many;
I can add scarves, jewels, pins to any.
Change my look with a gambler, fedora, or cowboy hat;
They are conversation starters and I like to chat.
I like black and white the best;
And red would be third over the rest.
Not quite old enough to be a red hat lady yet;
But old enough to know in my ways I am set.
One day I will write about what goes on in the mind under the hat.
But you are going to have to wait just a little longer for that.
Got a lot more things to learn and more living to do;
The hats are part of me and to my own self I am true.

To my beautiful niece: *Jordan Elizabeth Sumpter 2012*

I have watched you grow, listened to you breathe, held your hand through many things.
And now it is time for you to spread our wings.
You have held my heart as my sunshine girl that always makes me smile.
If only you could stay my little girl for more than just a little while.
As the years have gone by I have spoiled you, mentored you and above all loved you,
And encouraged you to do the best you can at whatever you do.
My arms are always here for you to run into for comfort, a hug or to ease your pain.
No matter what the need you will be safe and protected from the world until on your feet again.
I will always be here to wipe your tears and even laugh or cry with you.
Just remember to be who you are and to yourself always be true.
Spread your wings and reach for the stars, moon and sun.
And you will go far, so take off little girl and go for a life of joy and fun.
But always remember that wherever you may roam.
There are always open arms here and a place you can call home.

Under Pressure
© February 2018

The world is moving full speed ahead.
We are being dragged along instead of being led.
Under pressure to get it done right now;
Or we miss out on something and we don't why or know how.
Our heads appear to be buried in the sand.
We are searching around trying to find a helping hand.
Some people don't want to know, see, listen or hear.
Those things are changing and that is being made so clear.
Under pressure to keep up with the fast moving pace.
Chasing the dream that is now lost without a trace.
Trying to keep our lives on an even keel;
What is happening around us does not seem real.
Under pressure to stay ahead of the game.
Life as we know it will never be the same.
The older we get the faster it seems to go by.
Time is of the essence to catch up and we have to try.
The younger you are does not mean things won't change for you.
You blink, turn around and changes have happened to you, too.
Under pressure to make the best of the world has to give.
We have to find time to just slow down relax and just live
So many things are wrong that we have to make them right.
Under pressure it just makes people want to step up and fight.
Words are spoken that sets tempers on fire.
Some of the consequences of our actions are even dire.
Under pressure to make the best changes for all;
(Continued)

*It is the duty of everyone to help not just one man on call.
Under pressure to work together as a team that can win;
We need to step up and speak up but are not sure how to begin.
Those who are watching the world go by thinking nothing affects them
They are going to be surprised when it sneaks up and it all seems grim.
Under pressure and a race against the changes and time;
Technology and media of all kinds bring to the forefront the hatred and crime.
From days gone by when we did not know what happened all around:
To knowing too much from the moment our feet hit the ground.
Under pressure knowing that it is all so real;
We don't always know what to say or how to even feel
But one thing is for sure whether you believe it or not,
We have something in common that many seem to have forgotten.
Under pressure we all have the one place we can turn and we can pray
We have our heavenly father who will listen to what we have to say
We all human and no one is perfect, not even one.
We are all children of God when all is said and done.*

Talk To GOD

*I talked to God today about things on my mind.
It seems prayer is the best way to unwind.
I asked him to make the world a safer place;
To help others be kind and work together as a human race.
I asked him to bless the ones close to my heart;
And give them a good life as they play their part.
I told him I had faith and believed in the word.
That I had read his book and the words I had heard.
I try to live by them and be the person he wants me to be.
I try to show others goodwill by actions and what they see.
I asked him to forgive me for the things I have done wrong.
Even though I try, sometimes my intentions don't always hold strong.
I sometimes forget and say and do things I should not:
But he already knows this even though they are things I forgot.
I asked him to show me the way to not let others bring me down:
To help me look the other way when I don't want to turn around.
I asked for him to bring peace of mind, heart and soul;
So I could think clearly and once again be whole.
I talked to him about so many things that I hope he hears.
I need to know he is listening so I can have no fears.
I talked to God today and it brought tears to my eyes:
That I need to talk to him more often than I realize.
I asked for the strength, comfort and the will to get through the day.
I kneeled, bowed my head and started to pray.
(Continued)*

And yes, I talked to God and felt his presence by my side.
I have handed over my problems to him to be my life guide.
I know his is with me even though I sometimes feel alone and lost.
He is my source of love as he paid the ultimate cost.

Changing History
October 2017

When the world is spinning so out of control;
And we watch helplessly as those around us become so bold.
When people tear down all that you build:
Not caring how long it took and the needs it filled.
When it seems some in the world is all about leaving their own mark;
Not worrying about how it changes history and turns things dark.
Are they looking to just make their own names known?
While changing the scene of life happenings with memories that are now strewn.
What will be remembered in years to come, the past as it was then or will it all be forgotten and the stories different remembering when?
The tales to be told will be from a different place and different view.
Probably a story that changes it all and that they won't even remember you.
When love turns to hate and makes it hard to breathe in;
When good turns to evil and the world becomes about sin.
When friends become enemies and have no good reasons why;
Just to be followers of the next trend, no matter what it is they will try.
They cry and complain and want more to change around them.
But nothing can be done fast enough; they think change comes on a whim.
You can move and cover walls but the history remains the same.
(Continued)

But if it hidden out of sight, you think it changes the blame game.
You can be a part of anger and grief and know it hurts your heart.
But to stop it from happening you don't want to play a part.
You sit on the sidelines and watch all the good and bad unfold.
There is nothing you can do to make a difference, or so you are told.
Evil versus good is all around and we just have to be alert with open eyes
The devil rears its ugly head in ways we all despise.
Some take aim and destroy all that is in their sight.
This does not make it better or make a wrong seem right.
Making a difference should be a part everyone one plays on stage.
To end the discomfort and the anxiety, the unhappiness and rage
The battle will rage on and we really won't understand it all; Just know God is the end game and he will make the final call.
Making a difference should be a part everyone one plays on stage;
To end the discomfort and the anxiety, the unhappiness and rage
The battle will rage on and we really won't understand it all; just know God is the end game and he will make the final call.

A World to Change
December 10, 2011

A world to change? What difference would it make?
And how much animosity and hate would it really break?
To find a way to do better things for good.
On all levels if only we would.
To change the world. What a challenge to meet.
It has to be compromise on all parts as it is a two way street.
To bring everyone together to the offer the best for all
Create a world that withstands any fall.
To change the world means a world of change to some goals.
We need to be one and act as a whole.
A changing world day by day as we live like it is our last.
Time rushes on and soon today is over and it is the past.
True believers know that change is going to come
Great news for those who look forward, but not so much for some.
When the world comes to an end someday
We should all be in accord.
Because when the world changes for the future,
We will be rising up to meet the Lord.
A changing world is already taking place
We will know why when we see the heavenly father's face.
He has all the right answers and they won't seem so strange.
It is a changing world we live in and it is really only his to change.

The World We Live In
June 11, 2011

The world we live in is so full of strife and misunderstandings right now
We want to change things but don't know how
How to stop fighting, war, loss, pain and grief
We need a moment to think, pray and breathe even if the moment is brief
We should take look around and see what others need
And in the world of destructiveness, we must to take heed
To observe the world around us and what is happening all around
From natural disasters to the things that are caused by man
As you, ask yourself if you should be the one to do what you can.
Do you take the lead and show others the way to a better way to live
Is now the time to take a step forward to be the one to
The world we live in is full of many options, jobs, homes and faces.
We make a name for ourselves in many places
We sit, we think, we laugh, we cry
We do things in life and have no reason why
We live in a world of people who are all different and unique in their own way
Are we careful with tier feelings and watch the words that we say?
It is just the world we live in that takes us on our journey in life till the end
The world we live in will always have a new adventure around the bend.
The world we live in will offers great things and takes us on a wild ride
(Continued)

Until we meet the treasures of another world on the other side.

What Happens
July 2017

What happens if the phone stops ringing and no one comes knocking at the door?
When the busyness around you just isn't there anymore?
When there is quiet, silence and nothing around.
When there are fewer ups and too many downs.
Those who promised to be by your side;
Have disappeared and have found so many ways to hide.
Broken promises to be the one to call when in need;
To get things done you still have to take the lead.
The loneliness surrounds and engulfs the heart and soul.
You are losing pieces of yourself that always made you feel whole.
What happens when you cry tears for no one to see or hear?
You are struggling to be strong and let know one see your fear.
What happens as time goes on no one still sees your pain?
You are all alone and isolated is how you feel over and over again.
Those who said it not to worry; you will always have someone around;
They are now nowhere in sight and nowhere to be found.
Age is really a state of mind they say and you want to stay in the know.
Keep busy and do your no normal things as you go.
But what happens when the body says I can't do this anymore?
When the mind is good but everything else hurts, aches, is pained and sore.
Will anyone take notice or will they just pass on by thinking all is well. (Continued)

Will they know what is happening even if you don't tell?
Time will go on and someone new will take over all the things you used to do.
But will they remember it and will all the " I'll be here for you" comments still ring true.
Will they know what is going on behind those windows and closed doors?
Will they pay attention, take note and even care anymore.
What happens when it time for God to call you home?
Will someone be with you or will be you all alone?
Take the time to make sure that those around you have care and love.
It will be worth it to those you help and to our heavenly father above.

Could it Be Magic?
1981

The soft wings of a butterfly so beautifully patterned:
He flies elegantly way.
The sun that climbs over the hill with brilliant color and warmth;
Burst into day.
The water that touches the shore and ripples over the shells;
Slowly sinks back into its sea.
The enchanting fairy that is so often dreamed about fades away into stardust;
Leaving it's magic behind.
The dancers on the stage become lost in a special world of music and applause;
The curtain falls.
The gingerbread house in fairytales so appealing to the eye;
Gets nibbled on and crumbles away.
The wind in the trees, blowing angrily;
Suddenly pauses and whispers a quiet song.
The snow covers the ground, a soft white blanket to the earth;
It melts away.
Could it be magic?
From the special wand, encircled by stars that dances magically;
Only in your dreams.

Take Away
1978

Take away laughter and you only have tears;
Take away happiness and there is only sadness
Take away sunshine you are left with clouds.
Take away smiles; you have frowns to greet you.
Take away love and hate becomes the emotion
Take away the emotions you are empty.
Take away the heart and you have no feelings
Take away the soul and you are nothing.

Two Faces
© July 2016

Liars, cheaters, deceivers, phonies and fakers;
All around us we are surrounded by takers.
We don't always see their true color until it is too late
They pull us in then turn on us and we quickly learn to hate.
Afraid to walk down the street and look anyone in the eye:
Afraid they will hurt us as everything going on really is a lie.
We hang our heads and see no one face to face.
We just hurry right by as we pick up the pace.
Too vulnerable to feel because they already fooled us in the past;
This kind of pain goes on with no time limit on how long it will last.
They think they know it all and try to push their thoughts on you.
You can't listen anymore and you just want to do what you have to do.
Two faces are what you see and what goes on behind someone's back.
So many wrong words and actions that you just lose track.
People are fooled and it is all for show,
But the truth is out there and you already know.
Sooner or later you will be revealed and people will just stare; Not sure what they are seeing but just knowing it is too late and they don't really care.
Fakers, phonies, liars, deceivers, cheaters all rolled into one.
You are discovered and suddenly left alone when all is said and done.

The Paper Game

The Mecklenburg Sun has been 30 years if my life so far this year.
Spent years in radio and newspaper and it then led me here:
I have been through a lot before finding my space back in my hometown.
I settled in for the long haul with my feet on the ground.
So many things I have photographed and so many ads have been sold;
So many things I have covered and so many stories I have told.
The miles I drove before technology came along,
Making things easier so that can't be wrong.
The things I have seen and the people I have met;
The things I have done and I am not done yet.
Known for my trademark, I am Lisa with the Sun, Lisa with the hat.
I represent the media no matter what I do or where I am at.
Ads, news, photos, radio, social media, and giving back
It is what I have been about almost 30 years and still on track
The one, the only that is out and about, I have covered so many things
Concerts, sports, fires, accidents, community happenings and whatever a new day brings.
Never a dull moment in this fast paced business that keeps you on your toes.
Each day is different and what it will offer no one really knows.
You can meet famous people, have meetings galore.
Long nights, deadlines, and tough issues but you come back for more.
Radio was fun and I spun many tunes over the years.
(Continued)

Songs and sounds have changed and will change again as the future near.
I put my own spin on my radio show and now do the same when I write.
They are thoughts, ideas and that are not necessarily wrong or right
Words are meant to express what you feel from the soul and heart
Sometimes they flow easily other times you don't know where to start.
I wear my hats and am hard to forget water so many years of being around
Paid my dues, worked hard for a living and don't know what is to play.
I am always on the job in my car, home, or wherever I choose to stay.
Some may come and some may go but I am constant in whatever I do.
I am what I am, dedicated, honest, hard-working and to my own self I am true.
A job does not define one, nor does a hat, or a paper with a name
No matter what the future holds I am in on how to play the game.
I am Lisa with the hat and I am here for a bit longer if that is God's plan
I will hold my ground and be harder to move because I am Lisa and here I stand.

Waiting on a Sign

January 2016

I am waiting on a sign that you are still around:
Just something to let me know that you won't let me down.
So many times you picked me up and made it all right:
I still need those moments to make me stand and fight.
Encouraging words and support through every life trial:
Praise and laughter and all triumphs celebrated with a smile.
Talking about everything and making time pass as we always do:
Never thought it would not last and how soon we would lose you.
I wait to feel your guiding presence as the old wives tail say:
That a loved one would be around as your guardian angel every single day.
I know you watching over me to see that I am safe and all is well with me.
I know your hand in God's hand is leading the way for me to follow and see:
The sign I am waiting for has been here along.
Your love embracing me from heaven is mighty, powerful and strong:
I just have to reach out and feel the grace of God from heaven above:
And I will know my sign from you is his grace and all abiding love.

Drama

Don't need anyone's drama, conflicts or problems around me
Got enough of my own so leave me be.
I know who I am and so does the good Lord above
It means that no matter what I am surrounded by love.
Don't need anyone to tell me what to do
I can handle my own problems, don't need you.
Stop aggravating the already raw wounds
They will heal on their own and someday soon
I can close you out and walk away.
This is not something that is going to haunt me every day.
Don't need the pettiness of someone else's misery being passed around
I am strong enough to keep my feet on the ground.
I am confident in what I represent and how I live
I have a lot to offer and a lot to give
So don't bother me with stuff that does not mean a thing
I am only interested in what being a good person can bring.
So get behind me and try to keep up with my steps as I move
I have nothing to be ashamed of and nothing to prove.
I am Honest and true and come from the old school
And I won't play your games and be made a fool.

Trapped

The walls are closing in around me.
The darkness in the tunnel is all I can see.
My mind is in turmoil as I struggle with time alone.
The quiet is so loud and the screaming in my head sets the tone.
Trapped in my mind, body and soul;
My thoughts run hot and then run cold.
Nothing is making sense and no matter how I try:
I can't find the answers and I continue to ask why.
Trapped in my own head with thoughts that won't go away
They don't stop and I relive them every single day.
How do I find peace and make it all make sense in the end?
It all came crashing down and I don't remember when.
It is all spinning around me in a circle of images in my mind.
Looking for answers but in the end what will I find?
Trapped in confusion as to how to get out of the cage:
How to make a difference move on and then turn the page
Trapped inside my own mind and the sounds keep shouting to me
To see a way out of the trap that has locked its door so I am not free
Trapped in all aspects of a life that feels like a tight grip on being sane
Run fast run and run far until there is no more pain.
Open your mind then open the door and let the spirits run wild and free
The trap is no more and all at some point will become as it should be.

Voices

*The voices in my head are screaming at me.
They want to be let out and set free.
They are wrestling with my inner thoughts in my mind
They know I am searching for a peace I won't find.
The noises are deafening and drowning out all other
sound: Words and screams scrambled all around. I can't
understand and it makes no sense
It is just making me nervous and keeping me tense
They need to calm down and come to a rest
While I try to get a handle on it and do what is best.
My head in my hands as the noises keep on rumbling.
Into darkness, it feels as if I am tumbling.
Hands on my head as I try to make it go away.
But they just keep thumping in my brain night and day. I
feel as if I am spinning like a whirling top
Please shut up and make it all stop.*

I'm Not Perfect

I am not perfect but I put everything I am into what I do and how I live.
I want to be the best I can and give all I can give.
I want to make a difference in the lives of those around me and do so with an open heart.
Whatever life asks of me, I want to do my part.
I am only human and I may make mistakes and miss a beat or two.
But the lessons I learn will send me in the direction that for me is true.
I live my life for myself and bother no one else with whatever it throws at me
I do the best I can and only ask things of myself and hope you see. I am not perfect. I cry, yell, hurt, speak, react and live life as a good person with flaws.
I think things through with too many thoughts and way to much pause.
I can vocalize with vigor or be quiet with still and calm.
I try to work with all and cause no one any harm.
I just want to be the person, who knows that she has made changes to her life that has led others to do the same. We only get one chance because this life we live is no game.
We can score a goal, a touchdown, make the basket or hit a home run.
I want to know that I have touched lives when my own living has been done.
I am not perfect and will never claim to be. I want to watch, Listen, learn and just be me. I want my heart to love and my soul to soar free.
I want to feel, breathe, dream and grow into my life; that is as it should be
Imperfections, misadventures, mistakes and all without a worry. (Continued)

It is what makes me who I am as **Lisa E. Clary**.

The Road
January 2015

How does one plan life as you walk such a crooked road?
The rocks dig into your feet as carry a heavy load.
The burden gets heavier with every step you take;
It doesn't matter how far you walk or how many turns you make.
There are twists and bumps and places to fall down.
In some places your feet may not always be on solid ground.
You keep moving forward but the road never seems to end:
Always another obstacle just around the bend.
You see only more paths that seem to lead nowhere.
How do you choose one to take you anywhere?
There seems to be no place to really go,
You just keep moving; to where you don't know.
The road just keeps getting longer; so far ahead of you.
How do you decide when to take a break and to know what to do?
Moving on, walking forward, leaving behind footprints, but not knowing where they lead.
As uncertainty and curiosity takes over and we don't take heed.
The ever winding road of life stretched so far out ahead;
We will never stop walking it no matter how much we feel dread.
It will keep us wandering as it is a part of how we live
We search for something we can't find, until there is nothing left to give.
Ahead and in sight the path in the road still continues to grow.
What really lies at the end of it; will we really ever know?

Heaven

The door to heaven is open to all those who believe;
It is a place to rejoice and never to grieve.
The pearly gates will swing open wide;
As you walk through with Jesus by your side.
Angelic voices will ring out through the land
As you are heralded with songs of harmony from a heavenly band.
Sun, moon, stars, wind, rain and day and night,
Fade way as he becomes the leader of way, the truth and light.
Touch the hem of the garment of the chosen one,
And ask for salvation in all you do and all you have done.
Love is all around as he reaches out his arms;
Protecting you and keeping you safe from all harm.
The holy light that shines and lights what you see near and far
Means he is the one that shows us the way, as he is the brightest star.
A gentle peace surrounds and encircles all his disciples and those who believe
Put your trust in Him and he will never leave.
Even when you think all in life is lost;
Look to the Lord because the key to heaven hung on the cross.

Is All Right With Your Soul?
2015

Is everything right with your soul today?
Have you made a connection with God in any way?
Is your heart open to believing that he loves us?
Unconditionally, without judgment, as long as in him you trust.
Faith is knowing that his answers are right for you.
Even if it means you have to question what you do.
Are you reaching out to ask for his help in time of need?
Or are you trying to carry a load that is heavy and take the lead?
Will you step back and walk behind in his footsteps and follow his road?
Will you walk the path where the seeds of life are sowed?
Will you let him guide you and take his hand as he reaches for you?
When he speaks the words of the Bible, will you hear?
Will you go forward and search out a life with no fear:
As you rely on him and believe that he has your interest at heart?
Will you say hear I am Lord; I will try to do my part?
Is everything right with your soul today?
As you kneel down and bow your head to pray?
There should be no questions about how he wants you to live
He is there to help you and will always have the love to give.
Hung on a cross where he was tormented and died;
He still has the power to walk by our side.
A spirit of Holiness and a beacon of hope and peace.
With him all is possible as we find a new lease.
A life that is tread on a path of gold
Believing a story that many times has been told.
(Continued)

*Holding on to God our Savior as he makes us feel whole.
Trusting that he is on hand and everything is right with
our soul.*

Looking for Answers
© *April 2018*

How do you stop the walls from crashing in around you?
When you have done everything you know how to do.
How long can you hide the pain that only you can feel?
Going through the motions like it is really no big deal.
Laughing and smiling like all is good and well;
Moving through it all so no one can really tell.
The world is throwing stuff at you with no end in sight.
How do you make it stop so it all comes out right?
The mental anguish plays hard on the mind,
As you struggle for answers you can never find.
No one looks past the surface to see what lies beneath it all.
They accept what they see and never make the call.
So wrapped up in their own lives they miss what is being shown.
To think later about how they didn't see it and wish they had known.
Hurting on the inside while putting on an outside show;
From feeling really high to dropping to the lowest of low.
The darkness takes over and the light fades away.
You reach far to find the strength to make it through another day.
What used to be bright and shiny is now rusty and dull.
The busyness of motion in life is now a frustrating lull.
The walls are closing in and trapping the body and soul
Fighting for a way out to once again feel open and whole.
It is making a stifling shadow of what one used to be.
How do you find away a way back to a life that is free?
How do you pray for answers to questions you don't know how to speak?
Will it be sign of giving up and showing that one is weak?
How do you ask for something when you don't which way to go?
(Continued)

Will you recognize when the signs are shown and will you even know?
Do you have the faith to believe that God will listen and hear?
Will you turn it all over and go forward without any fear
Do you give it all up as you try to fulfill your needs?
Do you trust enough to wait and see where he leads?
Do you rely on others who don't look close enough to see?
That you are just making the little effort it takes to just really be.

When Times Are Tough

Times are tough, but I can still take the ride;
As God will get me through because he knows how hard I tried.
I have held my own, and stood my ground on steady feet.
I know who holds on to me and the devil can be beat.
My faith in God has got be my sustaining strength in life;
He can get me through financial woes, health issues and other major strife.
I am stronger than whatever tries to weigh me down and hurt me.
I just hold my head up, look to the heavens and see what I see.
A hope, a prayer, a miracle, and hand for me to grasp:
To pick me up, hold me and in his love I will bask.
Nothing I can't handle, because he said it was so.
And with that tiny seed of faith, it is the truth that I know.
In front of me, beside, me, behind me, I feel he is always there.
Listening to me, guiding me and granting me an answer to a prayer.
I am still holding on even in tough times and I am not the only one.
Life is taking a different direction for us all when all is said and done.
I am at peace even in my turmoil because my faith holds strong;
Because my belief in the heavenly father can't be wrong.
He is there for my tears, laughter and whenever I call.
We are in this thing together, my God and I, for the long haul.

The Outcome

In a world filled with hate how do we learn to love again?
We should not be causing others turmoil, fear or pain
We are a country where soldiers fought and died for us to be free:
Even if that means different thoughts, ideas and agreeing to disagree.
We should not spew hate or retaliate because two wrongs don't make it right.
We need to stop the eye for an eye before there is no end in sight.
We should love this land and all it stands for including those who fight for peace.
We need to hold our own and see that obstruction and violence will cease.
Law enforcement should be respected as we rely on them every day.
When they leave home family members are left to worry and pray.
Do we stand behind closed doors or hide behind the blinds to keep out the sin?
Do we wrestle with the evil and play a game with lives in a battle we may not win?
God is the ultimate protector and we need to be in touch with his saving grace:
Whether fighting the devil or another enemy up close and face to face.
Does land of the free and home of the brave still hold true?
Or do those words now mean nothing to you.
See the injuries, feel the danger, hear the heart wrenching cries.
Turn your heart to God and pray before we are overrun by lack of morals and too many lies.
We need to stand by each other as a country of humans who seek the same thing. (Continued)

Peace for all, love of mankind and a home country where we can let freedom ring.
We must be of one mind and strive for the same goals before it is too late.
If we don't pray and ask for forgiveness, will we seal our own fate?
Take the time to think about what you say or do as no one wants to that their life does not matter.
It is time to be at ease, quiet the storm and stop listening to all the idle chatter.
We are one nation, under God and he sees us as all the same until you choose a different road.
But even then you won't be judged by him until at the heavenly gates when you pay what is owed.
We should not judge lest we be judged by the greater one.
He has the final say when all is said and done.

The Life I Lead

*The life I lead is one of uncertainty at times
But isn't everyone's?
I look back to think, to remember what I have done.
Did I do the best I could in all things
Do I now accept life no matter what it brings?
Do I question the big picture and the all-around plan?
In the life I lead, am I doing all I can?
Do I lead my life with a sense of purpose and pride?
Is there something I need to do that I haven't tried?
Is the life I lead one of compassion, thoughtfulness and well-being?
Is there more out there me, things I am not seeing?
Is there a hidden meaning in all the things I say or do?
Or in the life I lead, to myself, am I being true?
Are there changes that can be made to benefit all?
Will they have an impact whether big or small?
Is the life I lead one that makes a difference to mankind?
Do I try to be honest, sympathetic and kind?
The life I lead is one that offers laughter, joy, love and fun?
Have I appreciated it when all is said and done?
The life I lead is the only one I know how to live and share?
But in the end will anyone really care?
The life I lead I hope to fill with many more years
And face each day without any fears.
The life I lead is the one that makes me, who I am; the person you see
And until the day it ends, I will have to be me.
The life I lead is mined alone and I face it my way.
But I meet it head on each and every day
The life I lead is the path I take to find new things
And I will accept it all, no matter what it brings.*

Am I Worthy?
March 2016

Am I worthy Lord, of the mercy and grace you show to me?
As I strive to be the person you created me to be.
Am I worthy Lord, to call on you in time of need?
As I bow in prayer daily to let you take the lead.
It seems I ask a lot of you as I keep you in my heart.
Sometimes I need to talk to you but don't know where to start.
You can see what is in store for my life as I search for my way.
The road may get rocky and take turns but I will not stray.
Your path is before me and I just have to follow your steps.
Trust in you and your plan no matter how many tears I have wept.
Am I worthy of your trust Lord, as I seem to cry out to you a lot these days?
I need to believe in you and make sure I live my life in all good ways,
Am I worth, Lord, to even question what you may have in store for me.
I have to know that it will be alright and demons will hear your voice and flee.
My heart cries out in the night for peace and a calm soul;
Even when I know that leading me forward is your true goal.
Am I worthy Lord, of being a one of your many sheep?
Even as I am not perfect and stray sometimes and it makes you weep.
Am I worthy Lord of being picked up again and again and wrapped in your sheltering arms?
Even when I fail and submit to the devils charms?
(Continued)

*I am a child of God not matter how many times I may fail.
I know I will be returned home to safety as Satan fights
you to no avail.
Am I worthy Lord of knowing you are the Alpha and
Omega and the Holy One?
I will not stop asking am I worthy Lord, until my time on
earth is done.*

Fire and Ice
May 2016

I am fire and I am ice;
I can be sweet or not so nice.
I can run cold or turn up the heat;
I will fight hard to not accept defeat.
I will stand by you even when you push me down.
I get up to keep going and my strength will abound.
I can be hot and burn you to the core of your skin.
I can be freezing and make you chill from within.
I will be the one that makes you think;
Question your remarks, thoughts and bring you to the brink.
I will play with your emotions, heart, mind and soul:
I can feed your hunger or I can devour you whole.
I can make you bend, break and even fold;
I can release my grip and loosen the hold.
I can call your name and make you answer back.
I will listen to your cries and make you lose track.
I will mess with your mind until it seems strange to all;
I can hold you up or make you fall.
I can make you do things you don't want to do;
I will make it seem like all is good and true
Then I will pull the rug out from under your feet;
You won't know who it is that you will really meet.
I will make the ground under buoy seem so un-level.
You can't run and you can't hide because the one chasing you is the devil.
I am pure evil and I laugh as I have you in my grip.
You may wiggle and twist but I won't let you slip;
Until something else stronger comes along to end this fight;
I can hide behind myself and make you search to find the true light,
I am ice and I am fire.
Two faces of evil that makes me a liar. (Continued)

But wait! Something rises up to take over this quest and tries to free you.
God has a challenge to win this battle of wills that makes you do what you do.
He will conquer and take the lead in this game and he will win;
And that is when the reality of his power in your life will really begin.

I Am Lisa

Lisa E. Clary is my name and here I am again on a new day.
I hope to hang around for a much longer stay.
This is my life that started many years ago at CMH in South Hill.
I could not wait and came out backwards and early and was here by shear will.
That milestone birthday is coming fast, and I will celebrate my life with joy.
My parents loved me from the start even though my dad wanted a boy. Four girls and 20 years later they finally got a son.
That was it for my mom, she said enough of this, and I am now done.
We have had our moments as a family, but always stand strong and somehow 50 years does not seem so long.
More time is what we all need as we reach moments that make us think have we lived our lives right?
But those moments close in quickly when health or other issues become visible for some and sometimes a constant plight.
Things happen around us that suddenly open our eyes to what is going on for many in other parts of our world
And you want to step up and offer your best to help those in peril.
For those who reach out to others in time of need, you surround them with prayer, thanks and love
And look to the heavens for help from above.
We all want to be the best we can be, took a lot of years for me to finally see
I am happy to be here as the future days of all of lives fade into yesterday.
From the moment I was slapped at CMH for my first cry so they could see the tears.
(Continued)

Named after a soap opera star, I was not aware of any hardships or any fears. (Continued)
But life comes at us as we age, learn and grow.
Even at this age, I still don't think I am in the know.
But I know enough to see what is important to make life worth living.
It is what comes from the heart and the soul and what you are giving.
This life journey has truly taken me far and I hope the road always led me home to the town where I was born and where I now hang my hat.
Home is always where the heart is, where there is caring and love and support and we all need more of that.
I look forward to my celebration of my life in May, and hope to share with family and friends.
It truly is about where we are going, and not where we have been.
Love to you all as we continue all our journeys together.

Where Do I Begin

Where do I begin with the words I want to say to you?
As they come from the heart and how they ring true
My heart cries out to say how I feel inside
But I am held back because of fear and pride
Do I dare make it known that feelings run deep.
Or is it my burden alone and my secret to keep.
I have tried to show nothing and hold it in
And it so hard to go back where you have already been.
To love and be loved is all we really seek
But I can't hold on to it as I am too weak
We all search for it in our lives in many ways.
We seek validation, love and praise.
Where do I begin and what do I say to change it for all
I am too afraid to recognize it as I am afraid of the fall.
I am still chasing something that eludes me.
I guess it is what it is and will be what it will be

On The Job

It has been 25 years at The Mecklenburg Sun;
And there have been so many things I have done.
I started January 1, 1989, it was snowing and cold, but I trudged through;
Totally embraced by all in the town as I went out and got to know you.
Covered many events, way too many to count.
And learned something new from all of them, there is no doubt.
I have covered every kind of meeting you can think of: many hours of taking notes
Writing, transcribing, reading, listening and getting quotes.
There have been concerts, dinners, political events, and meeting some famous people too;From various singers, writers, politicians, public figures and more I have been privileged to meet a few
I got married, moved around, divorced and never missed a work beat;
Had a few illnesses, and a few setbacks but I won't admit defeat.
Blessed by the Lord who is on this trip with me all the way?
I hope to be able to keep doing a job I love each and every day.
I joined lots of groups and gave of my time and my heart
I want to give back and feel I am doing my part.
I have learned about so many things just by doing by talking to you.
Interviews, photos, questions, answers are all a part of what I do.
I have learned about others and told stories of how they live;
I am blessed to have a talent of which I can share and give. (Continued)

I have sold many ads to help bolster business for my clients; all whom are now my friends.
I have worn many hats, dressed up, dressed down and covered many trends.
I drove many miles and traded many cars before modern technology gave me a break.
It now goes to the office quickly no matter what photo I have to take.
I never thought I would be President of anything and that changed over the years; South Hill Chamber President, South Hill Revitalization and Lions and Rotary challenged my fears.
Media and promotion is my passion, whether radio or newspaper, the spoken or printed word.
It has truly been a great ride, although after all these years it seems a bit blurred.
Where will the next 25 years take me? Only God knows for sure.
I will face the future with whatever he asks me to endure.
Now if have to end before this turns into a tome.
But Lisa, the hat lady, is glad that she is in South Hill, a place she will always call home.

What's Going On Around Me?

*My heart is sometimes overjoyed and filled with love
And some days it hurts from anger and pain.
I don't know why others want to bring you down
What do they have to show for it and what do they gain?
Life is hard for all around us and we need to be treated with care.
We don't need extra problems and stress.
We just need someone next to us to just be there.
I watch others wander through life and wonder what they think.
How do they feel about those around them each day?
But they seem in a day dream, and stare into the world without a blink.
Are there any feelings or are they just going through the motions?
Automatic reactions to what is going on around them:
No feelings, thoughts or emotions.
My heart is sometimes filled with love, calm and peace
And sometimes it is filled with turmoil and grief
Sometimes I want to give it all away
Just to get my own relief.
But is there any such thing out there close enough to touch, reach and feel.
For all those around us are having the same kind of life;
It seems all such a blur, all automatic and so surreal.
I am taking the steps to move forward and keep life on an even keel
While those around me are pushing and shoving and sending me to another place.
The want to beat back the same fears and aggressiveness in today's world we all face.
Where are we going with our hearts filled with so many emotions and our heads in a different place?
I am waiting to find my comfort zone for my heart soul and mind. (Continued)*

All bringing me to a place where I want to be.
Just where that is going to lead, I have to wait and see.

Will I?
2017

Will I be remembered when I am no longer here?
Will you remember my name and hold it dear?
Will I be thought of with love in your heart?
Will I be just a small piece of life that played a part?
Will my accomplishments be remembered as part of I was?
Will I be mentioned now and then just because?
Will I have left something that makes you smile?
Will you shed a tear for me every once in a while?
Will I have made a difference with something I have done?
Will I have been the person that maybe changed just one?
Will I have been the person that someone could admire?
Will I have been someone that would work to inspire?
Will you remember things I did or said?
Will you move past what I worked for instead?
Will you forget my mannerisms, my thoughts, and my face?
Will other people become more important and fill my place?
Will you honor me and hold the life I lived close?
Will I just be a short term memory for most?
Will I be remembered when my life on earth is done?
Will you realize that my new life in heaven has just begun?

Christmas is Magic!
December 2017

The magic of Christmas is believing in something that you can't really see.
It is a feeling that can't be explained you just let it be.
The knowing that Santa and the elves are hard at work on toys;
To find them under the tree makes for better little girls and boys;
They know there is something that is just in the air:
The colors, the sights, the sounds, the sense that people care.
The songs, the smells, the laughter, the possibility of snow
Makes for a season of joy that brings people together wherever they go.
The love that we feel runs even more deep at this time of year;
As we all gather around to bring each other good cheer.
The tree, the presents, the children running around;
Excitement and wonder; they now know no bounds.
But the real meaning of Christmas is the birth of the baby wrapped in swaddling clothes.
No room at the inn they traveled a far; no time to waste, no time for woes.
The shepherds watched their sheep and an angel appeared with good news
For unto you a Savoir is born this night and will be your guide if you so choose.
In a manger he lay as three wise men followed a star to find the king:
Each had a special gift that they were to bring.
Gold, frankincense and myrrh they placed near his humble bed,
As they rejoiced to be near him at Bethlehem where they were led. (Continued)

The ruler, the Lamb of God, the great I Am and Lord of all.
He will never forsake you and will always heed your call.
This is the time of year when we all should rejoice;
Call out His name at the top of our voice. T
The real meaning of Christmas is the bible story we all know.
It has been told d many times from days long ago.
Christ our Lord was born on Christmas day;
A beacon of hope to guide us on our way.
We follow his path and his steps lead us to his heavenly throne.
This is our new home and resting place and we will never again be alone.

Where I Live
©2013
South Hill, VA
American Hometown

South Hill, VA is a great place to call home at the end of the day.
No matter what you need people will help and go out of their way.
Friendly, smiling faces, handshakes, waves, kind words and more will greet you.
Civic organizations, churches, military groups, and businesses, too.
Small town America with picture postcard scenes on the streets:
Welcoming visitors to music events, theatre, festivals, always somewhere to meet.
Proud of our tobacco heritage and how far we have come from days past.
Where industry, retail growth, tourism and the technology era is growing fast.
A town of hard working folks who make great things come together for the best.
Leaders who take charge of changes and put new things to the test.
A mixture of young and old who merge to help meet the same goals:
No matter what needs to be done, they all play their roles.
Parks for children to climb, play, swing and run,
Fields of green for batters up, touchdowns, goals, and more game time fun.
Restaurants, stores, offices, banks, markets, and schools meet community needs.
   Places to visit, shop, socialize, and groups that specialize in doing good deeds.
A great place to work, play and live. (Continued)

A proud little town with a lot to give.
A place where the heart, soul and mind can settle down.
South Hill is the place you want to call your hometown.

He Took Our Place
May 2017

As he hung from the cross with nails in his hands and feet,
He cried out only to his father that he was ready to take his seat,
He hung there in front of all knowing some did not care;
But he was there to lift burdens and his body was stripped nearly bare.
He took the pain and suffering as his body was beaten and torn:
He felt the blood on his cheeks as he wore the crown of thorns.
His soul cried out as he paid the ultimate price;
He knew what he was doing when he made the sacrifice.
For those who would lie, cheat, murder and steal;
He knew the pain and agony of the torture he would feel.
The scars he would bare as he knew his wounds would heal in eternity.
He would be facing his heavenly father, the almighty deity.
Because when we are ready to enter his home and see what is there;
We will know that how he was treated was not really fair.
He will stand at God's right hand to motion us on through
No matter what we said or did, even though he always knew.
He would bless us all with his mercy and his grace,
As we realize the wonder of the man who took our place.

Money, Money

Money, money, it is all about the cash, the dollar, the big buck
You have to work hard to earn as it is just not luck.
All about the green or coin in any form today
It is all we think about and nothing gets in the way
The richness that we seek is not about filling our soul
We all search for the dough to make us feel whole.
We think about it at an hourly wage to make it full week.
It is all about the bringing home the bacon that we seek.
Whatever we have is never enough
Makes us try harder when things are tough.
Those who have it make us turn the envy color of green
The envy overtakes us when our own times are lean.
We work harder and harder for the government take even more.
Or others who don't play fair and don't care what you are working for.
Dreams, food, a home, more things or just surviving each day.
Someone out there works harder to take it away.
Making a living is not what it used to be
Surrounded by those who are all about me, me, and me?
Those who have it always want more to make them look good.
Some give it away to make an impression, others because they feel they should.
The smack, the bank roll, the clams or whatever its name
You have to have money to stay in the game.
Work hard for a living but is just never enough to live.
Some sit it out and wait for others to give, give, and give.
No matter what you do, some just can't be on the same page
Money, money and more of it is all the rage.
Everyone is out for their own share and their own take.
(Continued)

*They root of all evil, but we have to have for own sake.
Money, Money, it will make or break you.
Just earn it honestly whatever you do.*

The Words We Speak
December 2016

The words we speak can change a life;
They can bring a smile or cut like a knife.
They make you think and echo how you feel:
You can't hide the emotion and what it may reveal.
You speak from the heart, soul and mind.
You hope to say the best words you can find.
The words we speak can make one feel many things;
Overwhelming emotions from the low depths to making the heart sing.
The words we speak can bring joy or pain;
They can be soft and soothing or filled with strain.
They can bring laughter or tears;
Calm your soul and bring out fears.
The words we speak can cause harm, hurt and grief.
They can also make life better and even bring relief.
The words we speak can mean so many things:
Be careful how we speak them and the feelings they bring.
Overwhelming thoughts and ideas spin around in our heads;
Think before speaking out loud so they are not words we dread.
The words we speak carry a great deal of meaning and weight:
They can change feelings, lives and even someone's fate.
Be careful of the tongue and how you lash out;
Be sure you know facts and what you are talking about.
Think before you throw words that break spirits and cause shame;
You should consider how you use them so others treat you the same.
The words we speak can carry a great value around;
Or cut to the bone, lift you up or bring you down.
(Continued)

Speak kind words and give praise for a smile
The words we speak can make a difference if only for a little while.

South Hill

The signs say welcome to South Hill "You Will like The View."
Come on in, as there is plenty to do.
Shopping, ball games, parks, great food and more.
Take a look around and take time to explore.
Farmers market, special activities and times to dance;
Just visit awhile and give us all a chance.
Colonial Theatre shows to highlight talent on stage:
A long time project that took years to turn the page.
Clubs, organizations and so many great people to meet
A better place is hard to find so South Hill is tough to beat.
Friendly faces, museums of farm life, dolls and trains.
You will want to visit them time and time again.
Picture postcard streets all lit up at night
The glowing effect of lights makes it all shine so bright.
Flags flying high wave gently in the breeze on a windy day.
They seem to summon you to say come on our way.
Visit us, move, work, or live here, no matter what you do.
South Hill is the town in which you will really love the view.

My Friend

A friend is someone who stands by your side through it all
There to hold u up or catch u when you fall
You know they are there behind you without looking back
They will give you advice and keep you on the right track
They hold your heart in a very special place
They will run with you guide you and a set a steady pace,
They take the time to talk to you when you call
Never giving you any reason to put up a wall
There is always trust, admiration, love and loyalty.
They treat you with respect and even like royalty.
They are the ones that make you laugh and smile
Things stay the same even when you haven't been together in awhile
They will give you that hug and hold you when you cry
They support your efforts in all that you try.
They know your secrets and thoughts and will never tell
They are the ones who know you all too well.
They have similar ideas, ethics, goals and you fit like a glove.
If you have even just one, you are truly rich with love.
I have the love of my family and they hold my heart each and every day.
They have my back not matter what comes our way.
Friends I hold close are also special to me;
They let me be just who I want to be.
I celebrate my treasures in life and give praise to God in prayer,
When I look to him in time of need he is always there.
I say thanks for what I have and count my blessings and try to pass them on
It is the right thing to do for a better world to dawn.
Take heart that good will someday triumph and overcome the bad. (Continued)

*I live my life to someday see the face of God and I will be glad.
But until that time, my friends, peace, love and faith can guide you,
To be a better person in all that God leads you to do.*

Thank a Soldier

Take a moment today to remember those who made the sacrifice of life:
Those who overcame the battle of dealing with war and all its strife.
So we may be free to do the things we do each day,
And speak the words we want to say.
To salute the flag, say a prayer, to shake a hand as a gesture of good will,
To thank those serving today and offer a moment of silence for those who gave
All and those who pledge to do so still.
War is never easy for anyone who wears a uniform to defend a land they love.
It is a mission of the heart as they pray for help and guidance from above.
To have the strength to fight for what they hold dear and true;
To defend God, men, and the red, white and blue.
Remember they do this for all us, even when it is fear they face:
To keep this the home they love and show there is no better place.
They hold to the beliefs and love of, country, home and land.
Always reaching out to offer others a helping hand.
Once a soldier, always a soldier and he will never hesitate to serve fellow man.
He does what is needed and always takes a stand.
And still today we all know freedom is never really free.
Thank a soldier today and every day and give them the praise they deserve and earn: For tomorrow is a new day and things could it take a very different turn.

Journey with God

*And God said: On this journey I am by your side;
Trust, believe and in my word you should have faith and abide.
I will walk with you so you do not falter or fall
When you are being tested by the devil, it is on me you must call.
When you are afraid, scared and having doubts,
It is on me you must rely because holding on to beliefs is what it is all about.
When things in life tend to be a burden and get you down,
It is in me that you gain your balance and where your strength is found.
When you want to cry, give up and feel all is loss;
Think of me when I was making my sacrifice on the cross.
I did it all for love so that you could have peace in your life;
By believing I died for your sins, bearing all your troubles and strife.
Through this journey I will carry you every step of the way.
Just call on me as you bow your head to pray.
I am your guardian, your angel, your guiding light.
No matter the problem I will make it right.
It may not be what you as, for but it will be what you need.
I have a plan for your life and you just have to follow as I lead.
I am beside you even when you think I am not there.
I hear you, I see you I am always aware."
And God said "I am the one walking beside you now and always. From now through eternity till the end of all days. Till I return to call my children home I am on this journey with you and you are not alone."*

The Power of GOD

Do you feel the power of God as he reaches down his hand?
To show us he is the almighty, to help us understand.
He is the creator and can take control of all things
Can you feel his strength in the wind, snow, rain, heat and cold?
Can you imagine this earth if his story had never been told?
Can you feel his touch as he guides you through it all?
Can you hear him answer when it is on him you call?
Can you see the beauty in things that every day he shows us?
Do you read your Bible and in its words place your trust?
Trials and tribulations seem harder on those who believe the word,
But prayer is always the right answer so don't be deterred.
Take a look around and see what God is trying to show the world.
He is the master, the alpha, omega with much strength to unfurl.
Do you feel the power of the Lord as the earth changes each day?
We see it happening around us but we sometimes lose our way.
Storms, diseases, crimes and other formidable beasts for us to fight.
But it is to bring your attention to him and doing what is right.
Destroyed once by water, next he promises a fiery end
We must keep our faith and to his garden we must tend.
Do you see that he is leading us ahead to reach that heavenly place?
That we may one day look upon his holy face?
(Continued)

Stand next to God and trust he is always there when you are in need.
He will keep you strong in his love and you just have to listen and take heed.
Hold him in your heart and remember he is at your command.
You just have to feel the power of God and reach out to take his hand.

The Devils Dance
May 2018

I feel like I am dancing with the devil today.
He is stepping all over me and is in my way.
I am trying to hold on even though things are tough;
But Satan is laughing with glee and making it rough.
Those evil eyes try hard to look into my soul,
But I am not giving in as I want to stay whole.
That long skinny tail, horned head and pointed ears
Sure are ugly but I have to face him with no fears
I may be dancing with the devil but God has my back.
He will lead my steps so that I may stay on track.
He can spin me around and step on my feet,
But I will keep moving and the challenge I will meet.
He may grab and pull and swing his twisted tail,
But God is on my side and he will not let me fail.
Dancing with the devil, he likes to put on a show.
I will not support him and he will have to go.
He will tempt and test me as he wants to be the best.
He won't quit and he won't let me rest.
He will run at me full speed ahead.
He wants me to jump high and fill me with dread.
He will give me a twirl and bring me into his firm grip,
But I know he is planning to make me slip.
He will lead the dance and stand so tall;
All the while he is plotting my down fall.
He is breathing hot on my neck and I feel the heat.
Get behind me Satan as my God can't be beat.
Scorching the floor and it is steaming with the fire,
To make me his puppet is his only desire.
Dancing with the devil as he thinks he has the upper hand;
But you can be sure in his clutches I will not land.
My Savior will take the lead and my dance will score high;
(Continued)

*The devil won't win no matter how hard he will try.
One last turn and the dance floor will become level;
God will take my place and he will be the one dancing
with the devil.*

Big Rig

*The stories this old highway could tell as the wheels roll;
So many big rigs on the road for adventures to unfold.
The driver sits high in the seat to peer through the windshield;
Just watching to see what the next stop on the journey will yield.
Watching other drivers dash in an out and speeding on ahead;
In a hurry to get somewhere; maybe home to rest in their comfortable bed.
His eyes are on the road as the music and CB radio blare:
His cigarette dangling from his lips as he has no time to spare.
He has to reach his destination and change up the load.
He has to make his time count as long as the wheels hit the road.
He drives through the night to the sunrise on a new day.
Only a short stop before he moves on because he can't really settle in to stay.
The road signs of life are for rest, food, drink and more;
Lead him to places that he has no idea what is in store.
One mile turns into two and the road gets to be a weary place.
He longs to see someone that greets him with a smiling face.
He does have family he does not often get to see.
He is making a living but home is where he would rather be.
Road side motels, rest stops, bars and diners are along his route;
As the semi rolls on and the landscape and Mother Nature is what it is all about.
The lonely ride is out in front of him in the form of thick black tar.
(Continued)*

*He has traveled many miles and he has traveled far.
He listens to breaker- breaker, what's your ten- twenty and ten- four.
Watch your speed; there is a bear trap and a Smokey at your back door.
Those air brakes can rumble and squeal but can't stop on a dime.
You have to give them plenty of room and give them enough time.
Those truckers keep on hauling what keeps the world turning.
They make those runs fast and keep the rubber burning.
They see many things and listen to what others have to say
But they have to keep moving on and have to go on their way.
Time is what they are facing as they meet a new deadline;
But soon they will make that last drop and all will be fine.
They will turn that rig around and again that long highway they will face
Alone behind the wheel this time he will keep a smooth and steady pace.
The white lines seem to go by slower as he continues to roam;
But this time that air horn will alert those waiting that the big rig has rolled on into home.*

I Remember When

I remember when the days went by slower and time stood still.
My childhood nights outside listening to the whippoorwill.
The swing set in my grandparent's front yard;
The days that everyone worked all day and labored hard.
Chasing lighting bugs and catching them in a jar;
Watching them blink before releasing and sending them far.
Picking buttercups and blowing dandelions into the wind;
Watching the big oak tree limbs in a storm as they started to bend.
Running through the garden hose as the water cooled us down;
Playing outside with jump ropes and bouncing balls on the ground.
The front porch swing and all the rocking chairs;
They did not have much but what they had was theirs.
Church on Sunday morning dressed in our best clothes and shoes;
We had the time to rest, relax and do whatever we would choose.
Sunday family dinners, saying grace and so many good things to eat;
Homemade biscuits, fresh garden vegetables and baked sweets were always a treat.
Neighbors and friends always stopping by or calling on the phone;
Seems someone was always around so you never felt alone.
Pulling the wagon with the siblings and playing in the dirt;
It was a time they did not really worry about us getting hurt.
Staying outside until the sun faded away; (Continued)

Bedtime prayers and being tucked in to wait for the new day.
Dolls, books and bikes and so many toys of all kinds;
It kept is busy so that was all that was on our minds.
I remember when life was simpler or so it seemed.
We had what we needed and about so many other things we dreamed.
What would it be like to go back where we have already been?
To a different life and time that we now recall as I remember when.

Keep the Faith

God, I am swimming as hard as I can but I am about to drown.
I feel as if my faith is lost and can't be found.
I am climbing that hill but I keep sliding back;
Grabbing the ledges as I go to hold me on track.
I am laughing at times when all I want to do is cry.
I can't get my footing no matter how hard I try.
I take two steps forward to only be pushed back four.
The devil is happy that I am knocking at his door.
I am praying and asking for your grace.
I have to keep the faith even it is just a trace.
I can't see or hear you God, but in know you are there.
I am praying on my knees that you bring me out of despair
I want to believe that you are guiding my way.
But it is so hard to be struggling each and every day.
The air I breathe is just being sucked right out me;
As I hold my breath trying not to doubt that you can see.
That river is rushing so much and I am about to sink.
I can't go around the mountain as it is harder than I think.
But you can move the boulders and clear the road
You can take my burden and help me carry my load
I just have to believe and put my faith in you:
(Continued)

Trust that you will guide me and carry me through.
My arms may get tired and my feet get weighed down:
My body may weary but my mind will stay sound.
I know I have to rely on my own beliefs;
As faith in my heavenly father will bring me relief
Hold on to faith and pray to stray strong
God has been holding on to you all along.
All in his time as it is part of his plan;
Until he plays it out we have to do the best we can
(Continued)
Swim through the waters with your head held high
You can make it across if you really try
Climb that mountain until you reach the top
Keep your faith strong because God's faith in you will never stop.

Just Words

They are just words that come from nowhere
Sometimes no rhyme or reason but they are there
Words in my head that keep spinning around
I just have to get them out and write them down
Words on paper mean nothing to so many
If I don't write them down if there is peace I won't see any.
They just start with a thought or a line
And then so many other things come to my mind
They may be jumbled and mean nothing at first glance
But I have to play with them and give them a chance
They become something that reflects something in life
Some may be funny and some will cut life a knife
They are just random, one liners, and more may commence
But put together they will finally be something that actually makes sense
I write them all down before they get away from me
Go back later to translate and see what I see
(Continued)
Then I start to rearrange, change, and run through my head and rhyme
It sometimes takes a few days and some will take very little time
I can't explain it; it is just something I have always done.
(Continued)

It is my stress reliever and maybe a little bit fun.
I turn them into poetry and that all starts with word play
It all comes out into something I really want to say
Some may like and understand it and some may not
But I have to do it and give it all I have got
It is not for some and that is okay with me
They are just my words and I have to set them free
It does not matter where, how or the time of day
They are just there and want to have their say.
They are just words that clutter my mind whenever they want
If I don't use them they will continue to haunt
So, here you go, as I try to explain this blessing
These are my reasons so you don't have to keep guessing.
They are just words that come out of nowhere.
And I write them down and lay my soul bare
I thank God for allowing me to be able to share this talent with you.
I give him the glory in every word I write and all that I do.

*****

NOW THIS MUST COME TO AN END. THERE ARE MORE WORDS I COULD PRINT BUT THIS IS ALREADY A TRUE BLESSING.

I HOPE YOU FIND THIS BOOK TO BE DIFFERENT JUST LIKE ME AND THAT IS THE WAY I WANTED IT TO BE 'UNIQUE'

I AM FOREVER GRATEFUL FOR YOUR LOVE AND SUPPORT.

I SEND SPECIAL THANKS TO MY FAMILY AND FRIENDS FOR THIS OPPORTUNITY.

I AM HONORED AND HUMBLED. MAY GOD BLESS YOU ALL.

*****

****

THE CLOSING LINES AND THE LAST PAGE FROM UNDER THE HAT!

I TIP MY HAT TO YOU!
MY HATS OFF TO YOU!

****

About the Author

Lisa E. Clary was born in Community Memorial Hospital in South Hill, raised in Brunswick County, VA and has called South Hill, VA her home for over 30 years where she works for The Mecklenburg Sun as an Account Executive, Reporter and Photographer. She has spent of most of her life working in the media field including a two year stint at The South Hill Enterprise after graduating high school and a 2 year period in Louisburg, NC with The Franklin Times. She worked over 15 years with WLES Radio in Lawrenceville as an on air radio personality/DJ, and account executive. She also wrote and produced commercials for local businesses during that time. A Lawrenceville native, she knows the community and the people well in both Brunswick and Mecklenburg Counties and considers most of the people she works with friends. She has been writing since she was in school and poetry writing has been her hobby for many years and it being so personal she has been putting the collection of them aside or a long time. Recently she decided to post some of them on Facebook and she was also encouraged to send them to her South Hill United Methodist Church newsletter. Now she is sharing her thoughts, random words and poetry for others to enjoy.

Lisa is a member of the South Hill Rotary Club where she has served as President, Public Image Chairperson and International Chairperson, The South Hill Lions Club where she also served as President, Public Image Chairperson and Membership Chairperson. She is a Past President and Treasurer of The South Hill Chamber of Commerce and is a member of The Relay for Life Committee, The South Hill Revitalization Committee (served as president four years) Market Square and Farmers Market Committee and is a past member of the Community Development Association and The Friends of the R. T. Arnold Library. She is a former South Hill Ruritan Club member and also served on the former local South Hill Performing Arts Committee, Alzheimer's Committee and the American Heart Association Committee in the past. She works to promote her community any way she can and enjoys working with all the people that she comes into contact with from day to day. She has three sisters, a brother and one niece that she loves very much.

****

****

"There is always something going on under my hat and if writing and my words is mark I want to leave in the world then this is the time to do it.
 So now you have it:

Lisa's Lines From Under The Hat:

Thank you for your support!

Made in the USA
Columbia, SC
11 June 2018